TRIANGLE HISTORIES
★★★★★ ★★★★★
THE REVOLUTIONARY WAR

THE BATTLE OF
LEXINGTON
AND CONCORD

Lewis K. Parker

BLACKBIRCH®
PRESS

THOMSON
———★———™
GALE

San Diego • Detroit • New York • San Francisco • Cleveland • New Haven, Conn. • Waterville, Maine • London • Munich

For more information, contact
The Gale Group, Inc.
27500 Drake Rd.
Farmington Hills, MI 48331-3535
Or you can visit our Internet site at http://www.gale.com

Photo credits: Cover, pages 5, 7, 9, 17, 23, 24, 28, 30 © North Wind Picture Archives; pages 8, 13, 15 history pictures.com; pages 16, 20 © Historical Picture Archive/CORBIS; page 19 © Archiving Early America; page 26 © Bettman/ CORBIS

LIBRARY OF CONGRESS CATALOGING-IN-PUBLICATION DATA

Parker, Lewis K.
  The Battle of Lexington and Concord / by Lewis K. Parker.
    p. cm. — (Triangle history of the American Revolution series. Revolutionary War battles)
  Includes index.
  Summary: Describes the people and action of the Revolutionary War battles of Lexington and Concord, Massachusetts, in which the first blood was shed in the fight for United States independence.
    ISBN 1-56711-619-1 (alk. paper)
    1. Lexington, Battle of, 1775—Juvenile literature. 2. Concord, Battle of, 1775—Juvenile literature. [1. Lexington, Battle of, 1775. 2. Concord, Battle of, 1775. 3. United States—History—Revolution, 1775-1783—Campaigns.] I. Title. II. Series.
    E241.L6 P27 2003
    973.3'311—dc21   2002003788

Printed in China
10 9 8 7 6 5 4 3 2 1

CONTENTS

Preface: The American Revolution

Today, more than two centuries after the final shots were fired, the American Revolution remains an inspiring story not only to Americans, but also to people around the world. For many citizens, the well-known battles that occurred between 1775 and 1781—such as Lexington, Trenton, Yorktown, and others— represent the essence of the Revolution. In truth, however, the formation of the United States involved much more than the battles of the Revolutionary War. The creation of our nation occurred over several decades, beginning in 1763, at the end of the French and Indian War, and continuing until 1790, when the last of the original 13 colonies ratified the Constitution.

More than 200 years later, it may be difficult to fully appreciate the courage and determination of the people who fought for, and founded, our nation. The decision to declare independence was not made easily—and it was not unanimous. Breaking away from England—the ancestral land of most colonists—was a bold and difficult move. In addition to the emotional hardship of revolt, colonists faced the greatest military and economic power in the world at the time.

The first step on the path to the Revolution was essentially a dispute over money. By 1763, England's treasury had been drained in order to pay for the French and Indian War. British lawmakers, as well as England's new ruler, King George III, felt that the colonies should help to pay for the war's expense and for the cost of housing the British troops who remained in the colonies. Thus began a series of oppressive British tax acts and other laws that angered the colonists and eventually provoked full-scale violence.

The Stamp Act of 1765 was followed by the Townshend Acts in 1767. Gradually, colonists were forced to pay taxes on dozens of everyday goods from playing cards to paint to tea. At the same time, the colonists had no say in the passage of these acts. The more colonists complained that "taxation without representation is tyranny," the more British lawmakers claimed the right to make laws for the colonists "in all cases whatsoever." Soldiers and tax collectors were sent to the colonies to enforce the new laws. In addition, the colonists were forbidden to trade with any country but England.

Each act of Parliament pushed the colonies closer to unifying in opposition to English laws. Boycotts of British goods inspired protests and violence against tax collectors. Merchants who continued to trade with the Crown risked attacks by their colonial neighbors. The rising violence soon led to riots against British troops stationed in the colonies and the organized destruction of British goods. Tossing tea into Boston Harbor was just one destructive act. That event, the Boston Tea Party, led England to pass the so-called Intolerable Acts of 1774. The port

4

of Boston was closed, more British troops were sent to the colonies, and many more legal rights for colonists were suspended.

Finally, there was no turning back. Early on an April morning in 1775, at Lexington Green in Massachusetts, the first shots of the American Revolution were fired. Even after the first battle, the idea of a war against England seemed unimaginable to all but a few radicals. Many colonists held out hope that a compromise could be reached. Except for the Battle of Bunker Hill and some minor battles at sea, the war ceased for much of 1775. During this time, delegates to the Continental Congress struggled to reach a consensus about the next step.

During those uncertain months, the Revolution was fought, not on a military battlefield, but on the battlefield of public opinion. Ardent rebels—especially Samuel Adams and Thomas Paine—worked tirelessly to keep the spirit of revolution alive. They stoked the fires of revolt by writing letters and pamphlets, speaking at public gatherings, organizing boycotts, and devising other forms of protest. It was their brave efforts that kept others focused on liberty and freedom until July 4, 1776. On that day, Thomas Jefferson's Declaration of Independence left no doubt about the intentions of the colonies. As John Adams wrote afterward, the "revolution began in hearts and minds not on battlefield."

As unifying as Jefferson's words were, the United States did not become a nation the moment the Declaration of Independence claimed the right of all people to "life, liberty, and the pursuit of happiness." Before, during, and after the war, Americans who spoke of their "country" still generally meant whatever colony was their home. Some colonies even had their own navies during the war, and a few sent their own representatives to Europe to seek aid for their colony alone while delegates from the Continental Congress were doing the same job for the whole United States. Real national unity did not begin to take hold until the inauguration of George Washington in 1789, and did not fully bloom until the dawn of the 19th century.

The story of the American Revolution has been told for more than two centuries and may well be told for centuries to come. It is a tribute to the men and women who came together during this unique era that, to this day, people the world over find inspiration in the story of the Revolution. In the words of the Declaration of Independence, these great Americans risked "their lives, their fortunes, and their sacred honor" for freedom.

The Minuteman statue stands in Concord, Massachusetts.

5

Introduction:
"Lay Down Your Arms...
and Disperse!"

★ ★ ★ ★ ★

Throughout the eastern Massachusetts countryside, the warning had been sounded. At the first sounds of alarm, farmers, craftsmen, shopkeepers, and their families had stirred from their sleep.

Late on April 18, 1775, regiments of British soldiers had left Boston and headed for Lexington and Concord. The word spread, and before daybreak on April 19, about 130 citizen-soldiers—militiamen—had assembled on the village green—a grassy triangle in the middle of town—in Lexington. The militia, called minutemen because of their ability to assemble at a moment's notice, had trained nearly a year for this possibility. Along with their commander, Captain John Parker, they listened for the sound of the redcoats' tramping boots.

For hours, the men waited in the darkness, but the British did not arrive. After a while, some of the men returned to their homes, while others spent time at the tavern. The captain told them to assemble on the green when they heard a drumroll call to arms.

Few men, including Parker, expected violence from the British. After all, everyone knew they were on a mission simply to arrest John Hancock and Samuel Adams, and now both men were preparing to leave the village. They would be gone before the British arrived.

About five o'clock in the morning, almost 700 British soldiers marched into Lexington. The militiamen were outnumbered 10 to one. Parker attempted to steady his men before the frightening sight of the redcoats. Then a British officer called out to the men who had reassembled on the green, "Lay down your arms, you damned rebels, and disperse!"

The odds were plainly against the militia, so Parker ordered his men to fall out and go home. As the British column advanced across the green, the militiamen moved back.

Suddenly a shot rang out. The British soldiers, in formation, fired a volley point-blank at the militiamen. As they ran for cover behind walls or by the corners of houses, the Americans returned the fire. The British commander yelled for his men to cease fire, but no one heard him. They did not stop their frenzy of fire. When the Americans tried to surrender or run away, the British soldiers used bayonets on them.

Finally, a drummer sounded the signal for cease-fire. Within 15 minutes, eight Americans had been killed and about a dozen wounded. The British soldiers gave three shouts of victory. The first blood had been shed in the Revolutionary War.

The first shots of the American Revolution were fired early on April 19, 1775.

7

British Spies

★ ★ ★ ★ ★

By 1774, about 4,000 British troops were stationed in Boston, Massachusetts, a town of nearly 20,000 people. In June—six months after the Boston Tea Party—Boston's port was closed by the British. Americans were not allowed to ship goods out of Boston, and no ships, except British warships, were allowed to enter. Once again, as had been true for almost 10 years, the British Parliament was pushing the colonists of Massachusetts to the limits of their tolerance.

Boston Harbor was one of the busiest seaports in the colonies.

Lieutenant General Thomas Gage, governor of Massachusetts Bay and commander of all British forces in the American colonies, gathered information during the winter of 1774–1775. A number of colonists were still loyal to the

Laws allowed British soldiers to search colonists' homes for any reason.

crown. Those colonists, called Tories, moved freely about the countryside. They were able to observe the militia drills and spy on the secret meetings of the Patriots—those who planned rebellion against the Crown.

From the reports of Tory spies, Gage knew that gunpowder and weapons were being stored in both Worcester and Concord. This was a clear violation of royal law, because King George III had ordered all American ammunition to be seized.

Gage's initial plan was to send troops to attack Worcester, about 40 miles west of Boston. Worcester had been a hotbed of rebel activity, and Gage's spies had reported that 15 tons of gunpowder were stored there.

During the last week of February 1775, Gage sent two men on a special spy mission. The spies were British officers—Captain John Browne and Ensign Henry de Berniere. Their mission was to walk from Boston to Worcester and back to Boston by way of Concord. Along the way, they were expected

9

to make a map of the area that noted the condition of the roads and identified places where American militia might ambush British troops.

The officers took with them notebooks to sketch the country-side. If anyone inquired about their activities, they were to explain that they were surveyors or laborers looking for work. They disguised themselves, as one later wrote, "like country-men, in brown cloaths and reddish handkerchiefs round our necks." Accompanying them was John Howe, a corporal, who was disguised as a servant.

The men took a route through Cambridge, and within a few hours they arrived at a tavern in Watertown. There, they decided to stop to eat. As the officers ordered their food, they commanded Howe to eat in the kitchen, because officers never ate with enlisted men. A serving woman noticed this strange behavior and recalled her recent job in a Boston tavern where British officers often dined. She recognized Browne.

As the serving woman removed dirty dishes from the table, the ensign commented that the countryside was very agreeable. The woman replied, "It is a very fine country and we have very fine and brave men to fight for it. If you travel much farther north you will find this to be true."

The party reached Worcester on Saturday night and stayed in an inn run by Tories. Because Sabbath began at sundown on Saturday, they could not travel the next day. One officer later wrote, "We could not think of traveling, as it is contrary to the custom of the country, nor dare we stir out until the evening because of meeting, and nobody is allowed to walk the streets during the divine service, without being taken up and examined."

On Sunday evening, they mapped hills and roads near Worcester before starting back toward Boston. At first, as the men walked the roads, villagers gathered to stare at them. Later, a snowstorm kept most people indoors. The soldiers continued through the storm and arrived back at the Golden Ball Tavern, another Tory inn in Weston. The next morning, their Tory host guided them back to Boston.

Gage was pleased with the report, but he did not want to risk sending a force of troops to Worcester. It was a great distance, and he feared the people would be alerted before his troops arrived. The report indicated that there was a river to cross through the marshes at Sudbury. Gage figured that American militia could set up a deadly trap there.

As he studied the map of the area, Gage decided that Concord was a more promising target. He knew that rebels often met there, and the village was only 20 miles from Boston, an easy march for his troops.

A few weeks later, in March, Gage once again sent Browne and de Berniere on a mission. This time they were to investigate the roads to Concord. On March 20, the men left Boston and walked through Weston on the Concord Road, the straight route from Boston Neck to Concord. Along the way, they noted that the road provided places where American soldiers could attack. They mentioned that the area was "woody in most places and commanded by hills."

When they arrived at Concord, the town was swarming with American militia. They asked a woman they met to lead them to the house of Daniel Bliss, a Tory lawyer and a leading citizen. The woman did so, and the officers enjoyed dinner with Bliss. As they were eating, the woman banged on the door. Crying, she said that she had been stopped by militia members who "swore they would tar and feather her for directing Tories."

A few minutes later a message arrived for Bliss. It was a death threat—Bliss would be killed if he did not leave Concord immediately. The British officers, who carried weapons, offered to protect Bliss if he wanted to travel to Boston. Bliss agreed to leave, and the three men started out for Boston.

★

Gage and George Washington fought together in the French and Indian War.

★

11

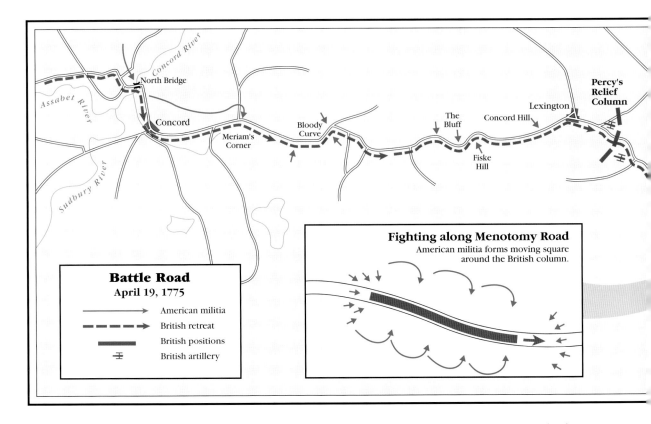

Battle Road
April 19, 1775

⟶	American militia
▬ ▬ ➤	British retreat
▬▬▬	British positions
⊥	British artillery

Fighting along Menotomy Road
American militia forms moving square around the British column.

Bliss led them on a return route that went farther north than their original route, through Lexington and Menotomy (present-day Arlington). It was a longer route, but the countryside was open and did not provide as many opportunities for ambush.

Back at Gage's headquarters, the officers recommended that British troops take the route through Lexington. Bliss also described the landscape of Concord, with the Concord River flowing between two hills. He mentioned the two bridges—the South Bridge and the North Bridge—that crossed the river. Bliss also stated that rebels had stored supplies in the town, such as cartridges, spades, iron pots, wooden mess bowls, salt, and rice. He added that gunpowder and cartridges were hidden on Colonel James Barrett's farm.

For Gage, the mission was taking shape. Concord would be the target.

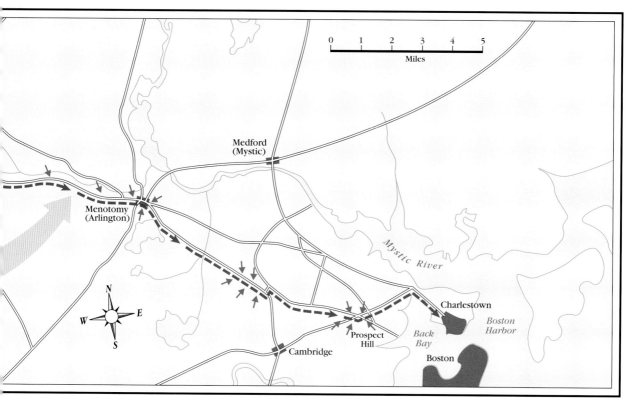

American Spies

Although Gage's men had safely scouted the country-side beyond Boston, the British commander was unable to move his huge force without alerting a network of Patriots. As the militia trained for a possible confrontation, other Patriots kept close watch on every move the redcoats made in and around Boston. One of the largest of the Patriot groups was Paul Revere's voluntary association of Boston mechanics, or workingmen. They held secret meetings at the Green Dragon Tavern in Concord. Revere later wrote:

> *"I was one of upwards of thirty who formed ourselves into a committee for the purpose of watching the*

Lieutenant General Thomas Gage was the military governor of Massachusetts.

The Battle of Lexington and Concord

movements of the British soldiers, and gaining every intelli-gence of the movements of the Tories. We were so careful that our meetings should be kept secret, that every time we met, every person swore upon the Bible that he would not discover any of our transactions but to Mssrs. Hancock, Adams, Doctors Warren, Church, and one or two other more. In the winter towards spring, we frequently took turns, two and two, to watch the soldiers, by patrolling the streets at night."

Secret Orders

Spying operations continued throughout late winter and into the early spring of 1775. Each side gained information about the other, and all of it pointed in one direction—confrontation.

On April 14, orders arrived for Gage aboard the H.M.S. *Nautilus*. Dated January 27, 1775, the orders instructed Gage to act immediately against "proceedings that amount to actual revolt." He was ordered to seize the leaders of the colonial protests, men such as Samuel Adams and John Hancock. In addition, Gage was ordered to take all weapons and military supplies away from the rebels.

It was apparent from the orders that Parliament had reached the limits of its patience with its American subjects. The earl of Dartmouth, a member of the House of Lords, stated, "It is the opinion of the King's servants, in which His Majesty concurs, that the first and essential step to be taken towards reestablish-ing Government, would be to arrest and imprison the principal actors and abettors of the Provincial Congress whose proceed-ings appear . . . to be acts of treason."

The British government believed that it would not be difficult to crush a rebellion in the American colonies. British troops had ended revolts in other parts of the British Empire, such as

14

Paul Revere

★ ★ ★ ★ ★

Paul Revere was a respected Boston craftsman.

Born in Boston in 1735, Paul Revere was the son of a French silversmith, Apollos Revoire, and Deborah Hitchbourn. He followed his father in the silversmith trade. When Apollos Revoire died, Revere, 19, took over his shop. Within the next 20 years, he became one of the finest American smiths. In addition to making silver bowls, utensils, and flatware, he made engravings such as cartoons, calling cards, and bookplates. His engraving of the Boston Massacre became one of the most well-known images of that event.

In the 1760s, Revere joined two political groups—the Sons of Liberty and the North End Caucus. As a messenger and an engraver of political pictures, Revere became a key figure in the movement for colonial independence.

On the night of April 18–19, 1775, Revere, following Dr. Joseph Warren's orders, rode to Lexington to warn Samuel Adams and John Hancock that British troops were leaving Boston. Although he was able to warn the rebel leaders, he was arrested by a British patrol before traveling further.

After the war, Revere, who had fought in one battle in Maine, opened a hardware store. He also built a foundry to make stoves, anvils, hammers, and pumps. His foundry was most famous for its church bells. Revere made 398 bells, many weighing as much as 500 pounds. He also established the first sheet-copper mill in the United States, and produced copper to cover the bottom of ships, including the U.S.S. *Constitution*. Copper from his mill also covers the dome of the statehouse in Boston. Later, he served as Suffolk County coroner and the first president of the Boston Board of Health. Revere died in 1818.

British troops, known as redcoats, had been used to put down revolts in Ireland and India.

Ireland and Scotland. The main mission of the British army, in fact, was to destroy rebellious elements, and British soldiers were well trained to carry out the task. Many experienced soldiers stationed in Boston had also served in Ireland and Scotland. Others had helped keep the peace and stop riots in England itself.

In response to his orders, Gage drew up plans to march to Concord and capture the supplies that were believed to be stored there. He laid out part of the route by water so his men would have fewer miles to march. Gage also believed he had an excellent chance to capture two rebel ringleaders—John Hancock and Samuel Adams. Spies had reported that the two men had left Boston to attend a meeting and were probably somewhere in Lexington.

The British government had already criticized Gage severely on several occasions for not arresting Hancock and Adams.

16

Samuel Adams

No American played a larger role in leading the colonies along the road to revolution than Samuel Adams. Born in 1722, the son of a Boston merchant and brewer, Adams graduated from Harvard College in 1740. A failure as a businessman, he devoted much of his time to writing newspaper pieces opposing the royal government. As a member of the Massachusetts assembly, he opposed the Stamp Act in 1765.

During the 1760s and 1770s, Adams wrote and spoke constantly about the British government's refusal to allow colonists a voice in their own government. His writing, speeches, and tireless activity attracted others to the cause of independence— including Josiah Quincy, Joseph Warren, and John Adams, Samuel's younger cousin.

Before the war, Adams established the Boston Committee of Correspondence and directed its activities from 1772 through 1774. He helped plan and carry out the Boston Tea Party, which became the pivotal event leading up to the war.

From 1774 to 1781, Adams was a delegate to the Continental Congress, and he became one of the signers of the Declaration of Independence. After the war, he was elected to the Massachusetts convention on the ratification of the Constitution, a document he refused to support because he was wary of a strong central government.

From 1789 to 1793, Adams served as Massachusetts's lieutenant governor under John Hancock. When Hancock died, Adams became the governor. He was elected three times before he retired in 1797. Adams, often called the "Father of the American Revolution," died in 1803.

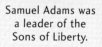

Samuel Adams was a leader of the Sons of Liberty.

Now he could end the criticism by destroying the weapons at Concord and capturing the two rebel leaders in one mission.

Bloody Lexington

By early April 1775, Samuel Adams and John Hancock had left Boston to stay with Reverend Jonas Clarke in Lexington. Clarke's wife was Hancock's cousin. Adams, Hancock, and Samuel's cousin, John Adams, intended to represent Massachusetts in the Second Continental Congress, which was scheduled to begin in Philadelphia on May 10.

On Saturday, April 15, Patriot spies noticed that the British warship *Somerset* moved to a position in Boston Harbor near the Boston-Charlestown ferry. Smaller boats were anchored near the mighty man-of-war. To the Patriot spies, this movement was suspicious. It suggested that the warship had been moved to protect troops, who were possibly planning to cross the Charles River in the smaller boats.

About 5 o'clock the next morning—a cold Easter Sunday— Revere rowed from Clark's Wharf across the Charles River to Charlestown. From there, he rode to Lexington, where he met Adams and Hancock at Jonas Clarke's home.

After the men discussed the possibility of a British raid, Revere rode to Concord, where he warned James Barrett of the likelihood that British troops would march to Concord to seize the Patriots' weapons cache. Quickly, Barrett organized carts and wagons to drag cannons, weapons, and ammunition to nearby Sudbury and Groton. Other supplies were hidden in the woods outside Concord.

Barrett then sent messengers to warn other towns to have their minutemen ready. When an alarm sounded, they were to march to Punkatasset Hill, north of the North Bridge of the Concord River, about a mile from the center of Concord.

John Hancock

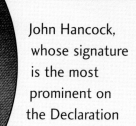

★ ★ ★ ★ ★

John Hancock, whose signature is the most prominent on the Declaration of Independence, was born in 1737. After his father's death, Hancock was raised by his uncle, a wealthy Boston merchant.

John Hancock

He graduated from Harvard and became his uncle's partner. When his uncle died in 1764, Hancock, his only heir, became one of the richest men in Boston.

In 1765, Hancock joined with the opposition to the Stamp Act. In 1768, he was elected as a representative to the Massachusetts legislature. When the Massachusetts legislature became a provincial congress in 1774, Hancock was elected its president and chairman of the Committee of Safety, which had the power to call out the militia to fight British troops.

In 1775, Hancock represented Massachusetts at the Second Continental Congress. He was elected president of the Congress, but, much to his disappointment, was passed over as commander of the Continental army. John Adams nominated George Washington for that position.

In 1780, Hancock was elected as the first governor of Massachusetts. He was reelected each time he chose to run for office. Because of poor health, he refused to run for office in 1785 and 1786. In 1787, he ran again and won in a landslide. While in office, he gave part of his salary to the state of Massachusetts.

During the process of ratifying the U.S. Constitution in 1788, Hancock kept his vote secret until the end of the proceedings. Then he offered his complete support only if a Bill of Rights was attached to the document. Like his lifetime comrade, Samuel Adams, Hancock was distrustful of a strong central government. The Bill of Rights was added, and the Constitution was ratified in Massachusetts by a narrow vote. Hancock died in 1793, at the age of 56.

PAUL REVERE

An early carving honored Paul Revere's ride.

Revere rode back to Charlestown. Once there, he met with Richard Devens, who directed the spy network in Charlestown, and Colonel William Conant, who was in charge of the Charlestown militia. The men arranged for signals to be given depending on how the British moved out of Boston.

If the British went by land through Roxbury Neck, militia from Watertown, Brookline, and Weston would be called into the fight. The men agreed that the British would probably be heading for Worcester if they took that route. In that case, Revere said, one lantern would be hung in the belfry of the Old North Church across from his home. That way, spies in Charlestown could warn the militia in Watertown, Brookline, and Weston.

If the British crossed the Charles River in boats, the men figured, it meant they would probably march to Lexington and Concord. If that occurred, Revere would see to it that two lanterns hung from the belfry. In that case, he planned to cross

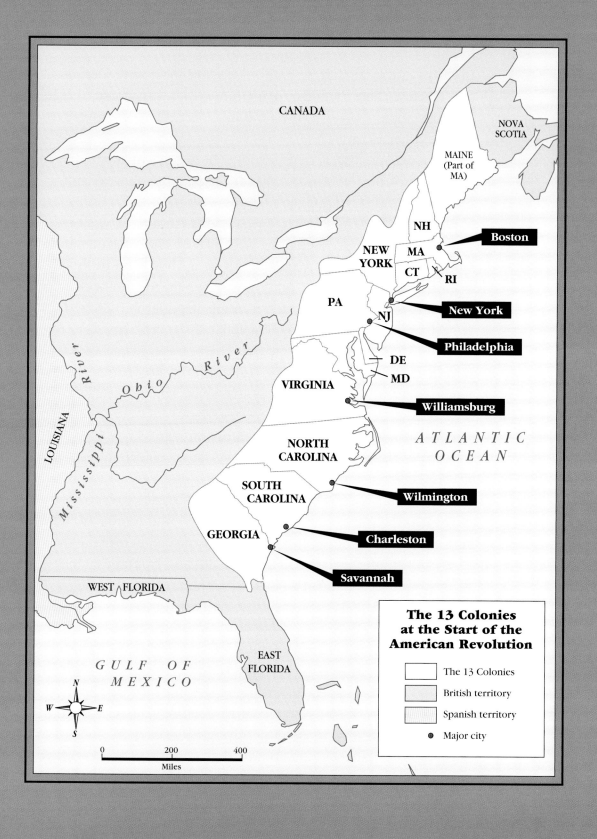

★

The weather was
unusually hot for early
spring in 1775.

★

the river in a boat that he had hidden and meet with Devens and Conant. They would provide him with a fast horse to reach Lexington and Concord. If he did not meet them, they were to send another rider.

There was no attack that day, but the arrangements had been made. All of Boston was on alert for the slightest movement out of the ordinary by Gage's troops.

On Tuesday, April 18, Gage was ready. About 700 well-trained, battle-hardened troops were placed under Lieutenant Colonel Francis Smith. According to plan, they were to leave from the foot of Boston Common, cross over to Cambridge by boat, and march through Menotomy to Lexington, where they would arrest Adams and Hancock. Then the redcoats were to continue the 17 miles to Concord. There, the soldiers were to seize and destroy all "Artillery, Ammunition, Provisions, Tents, Small Arms, and Military Stores whatever," the general declared.

The second in command of the mission was Major John Pitcairn of the Royal Marines. He was an excellent soldier who was respected even by the Patriots.

Plans called for the British to cross the Charles River at ten o'clock in the evening on April 18. They would march all night, pass through Lexington, and arrive at Concord before dawn. They were under orders to finish the mission by eight o'clock in the morning and return to Boston by noon.

That night, the British companies marched to the river. The crossing took two hours, and it was midnight before the troops finally arrived on Lechmere Point in East Cambridge.

Throughout the evening, Revere watched the British soldiers cross the Charles River. According to the Patriot plan, he then met William Dawes at Joseph Warren's home. Dawes was to ride to Lexington along a route through Roxbury Neck. He was to warn Hancock and Adams that the British were on their way to Lexington. Then he was to ride on to Concord and warn Barrett.

Revere was to ride to Lexington by going through Charlestown and Menotomy. He would give the same warning, and alert militia along the way.

As the crossing neared its end, and Revere was certain that the movement was not a trick, he sprang into action. He sent a friend to hang two lanterns in the belfry of the Old North Church. Then he was rowed across to Charlestown. At Charlestown Square, a horse was waiting.

He set off, crossed Charlestown Neck, and headed toward Menotomy. Suddenly, Revere saw two mounted British soldiers ahead of him. He wheeled around and took another road as the two soldiers chased him. Revere's horse outran the British horses, and he raced through Medford, alerting the militia. Then he rode on to Lexington, shouting and knocking on doors along the way.

Revere stopped at Clarke's home and pounded on the door. Sergeant William Munroe, in charge of the militia guard, answered, and Revere gave him the news. Within half an hour, Dawes arrived. After a short rest, Revere and Dawes started for Concord, and on the road outside of town, they were joined by Samuel Prescott of Concord.

Halfway to Concord, the three were stopped by a British patrol. Prescott jumped his horse over a stone wall and escaped. Dawes rode away, but fell off his horse after escaping, and went

The Old North Church was easily visible in much of Boston.

23

The call to arms went out as the redcoats left Boston.

the rest of the way on foot. Revere was taken back to Lexington as a prisoner. There, he was questioned before being released on foot.

Meanwhile, as April 19 began, the British soldiers left Lechmere Point and started on their march. They had to wade through the swamps of Willis Creek before they reached the main road. Most of the soldiers were soaked and covered with slime. They paused for several hours to dry themselves, which delayed the march.

By two o'clock in the morning, the British force was in full march on the road to Menotomy and Lexington. As they passed through the town of Somerville, Smith ordered the infantry not to take the wooden bridge that crossed the Charles River there. He feared that the soldiers' boots would make too much noise on the bridge and wake the town. Instead, he had the men wade through the freezing waist-deep waters. When they reached Menotomy, they formed a column with Pitcairn in the lead and Smith following.

The Battle of Lexington and Concord

About four-thirty, just before dawn, the British soldiers arrived in Lexington. On the edge of town, they heard the beating of a drum. Pitcairn knew that it was a military drum ordering men to assemble. He stopped his men so they could load their weapons. Then he ordered them to march at double time.

The infantry double-timed around both sides of the Congregational church at the southern end of the Lexington Green, where about 70 militiamen stood in two lines. They were not blocking the road to Concord, but their presence was a threat to the British soldiers. Many of the militiamen had been waiting for hours since they heard Revere and Dawes's warning. At that time, at least 130 militiamen had come into Lexington. Many of them had drifted off, and only about half that number remained, led by Captain John Parker. When the British appeared opposite the Buckman Tavern, Parker shouted, "Stand your ground. Don't fire unless fired upon, but if they mean to have a war let it begin here!"

At Buckman Tavern, the redcoats formed a column. Pitcairn commanded "Halt!" Then he commanded "Right face!" Now the British infantry faced the Lexington militia. Pitcairn ordered the militia to put down their weapons.

There was absolute silence. Finally Parker ordered his men to leave, and they started to move off. No one knows who fired the first shot of the war. British soldiers later said they saw a flash of fire from a militiaman's musket. Others said that a shot came from near the Congregational church.

A British soldier later stated that Pitcairn had shouted, "Soldiers, don't fire, keep your ranks and surround them!" Immediately after that, a shot came from the American side. Once the shot rang out, British soldiers fired volley after volley into the ranks of the militia.

The Americans fell back on both sides of the green. The soldiers followed, and charged with bayonets at the retreating

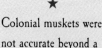

★
Colonial muskets were not accurate beyond a distance of 100 yards.
★

25

The Patriots were outnumbered and easily defeated at Lexington Green.

rebels. Jonathan Harrington, who was standing with the militia in front of his house, was hit in the chest and knocked backwards. He tried to crawl across the road, where his wife ran to help him. He died in her arms.

Jonas Parker was wounded by a blast from British guns. He recovered from the shot, loaded his musket, dropped to his knees, and fired his gun. Just as he did, a British soldier killed him with a bayonet.

Besides Harrington and Parker, the dead included Ensign Robert Monroe, who was killed as he crossed the green trying to obey Parker's order to leave. Caleb Harrington was killed as he tried to take cover in the church. British soldiers chased John Brown and Samuel Hadley into a swamp and shot them.

In minutes, the soldiers had chased the militia from Lexington Green. One British soldier was wounded. Although only a few of the militiamen had fired, eight had been killed and ten wounded.

Revenge at Concord

News of the battle at Lexington raced ahead of the British soldiers as they marched on to Concord. Suddenly the whole countryside was alert. Militiamen grabbed their weapons and dashed to Concord. The British arrived just outside of town at about seven o'clock in the morning. By then, more than 400 militiamen awaited them.

As the British marched into Concord, Smith divided his men into three groups. He sent three companies of infantry across the North Bridge past Punkatasset Hill toward the farm of James Barrett, the militia commander. Smith sent three other companies to the bridge to keep watch on rebel movements. He then ordered a third unit to search buildings in the center of town for weapons and gunpowder.

After they searched several buildings and found nothing, however, the frustrated redcoats in the third unit set fire to the

★
Adams and Hancock watched the battle from nearby woods.
★

27

Redcoats set fires
in Concord, which
enraged the Patriots.

courthouse and the blacksmith shop. The militiamen who had
assembled on Punkatasset Hill according to the plan saw the
smoke. They asked Barrett whether they should allow the
British to destroy the village. Barrett ordered his men to
advance, but told them not to shoot unless they were fired upon.

About 400 militiamen started down the hill toward the
British soldiers at the North Bridge. The British opened fire.
The first British volley was poorly aimed and missed its targets.
The Americans returned the fire, killing 12 soldiers—including
four officers. The heavy fire forced the British units to retreat
across the bridge.

Now that Americans held the North Bridge, they had cut off
the British companies that had marched to Barrett's farm. In the
confusion of battle, however, some of the Patriots returned to
their positions on the bridge, while others attempted to cross
the bridge and attend to the fire in the village. This group
scattered when the British troops who had gone toward
Barrett's farm raced back to the scene, drawn by the sounds
of battle. Thus the redcoats were able to cross the bridge and
rejoin their comrades.

The Battle of Lexington and Concord

By the time his troops were reunited, Smith had sent a message to Gage asking for reinforcements. He delayed any further action until more British soldiers arrived. By noon, when reinforcements had failed to arrive, Smith decided to march back to Lexington empty-handed.

At Merriam's Corner, along the road, the British fired at a group of militiamen. The militiamen did not hesitate to return the fire. From that moment on, the road to Lexington became a route of revenge for the militiamen.

Their fifes and drums silent, the British soldiers faced constant attack. American snipers picked off soldiers as they marched. Other militiamen ambushed the soldiers at every opportunity, firing from behind houses, barns, and walls. As the British continued to march, they left their dead and wounded behind along the road.

There was no letup on the fire. One company of militia replaced another and another along the way. As the British soldiers neared Lexington, discipline broke down. The redcoats panicked and began to run from the musket balls that whistled from every direction.

Only the arrival of three regiments of infantry—about 1,000 men—saved the British force from complete defeat. The reinforcements had brought a detachment of artillery. Taking a position on high ground, gunnery teams placed cannons on either side of the road. Six-pound cannonballs fired at the militia temporarily stopped the Americans.

The British soldiers rested for an hour, protected by the cannons and the reinforcements. At 3:45, they started the four-hour march to Boston. The commanding officer of the reinforcements ordered that American snipers should be killed, and houses that snipers fired from should be burned.

At Menotomy, where the land was flatter, the attacks began once more. Militiamen followed the British soldiers through the

Many redcoats were exhausted from the heat and lack of sleep.

29

The British forces panicked and ran from hidden Patriot riflemen.

woods and fields in flanks that fired at the column. By then, British soldiers had started to plunder homes they came across, and British soldiers fired into houses or set them on fire. Some militiamen were killed in hand-to-hand combat, while other Americans poured fire from the safety of trees or walls.

Near Cambridge, the Americans finally ceased the attack. The redcoats escaped into Charlestown Neck and returned to their camps. By evening, the toll of the battle was known. About 270 British soldiers had been killed and wounded, almost all on the retreat from Concord. About 95 Patriots were killed and wounded during the battle and pursuit.

No one knew who fired the first shot on Lexington Green, but the sound of musket fire echoed through the colonies. A revolution had begun. From that moment on, American colonists no longer bowed to the king of England.

The Battle of Lexington and Concord

Glossary

bayonet a long knifelike weapon attached to the end of a musket
infantry foot soldiers
militia regular citizens who serve in local military units
musket a shoulder gun used in the late sixteenth through eighteenth centuries
regiment a military unit smaller than a brigade and a division
reinforce in military terms, to strengthen a military unit by sending in fresh troops
Tory American who was loyal to the king of England
treason a violation of allegiance to one's country

For More Information

Books

Bobrick, Benson. *Angel in the Whirlwind*. New York: Simon & Schuster, 1997.
Fleming, Thomas. *Liberty! The American Revolution*. New York: Viking, 1997.
Kent, Deborah. *Lexington and Concord*. Danbury, CT: Childrens Press, 1997.
Whitelaw, Nancy. *The Shot Heard Round the World*. Greensboro, NC: Morgan Reynolds, 2001.

Web Sites

Liberty! The American Revolution
http://www.pbs.org/ktca/liberty/
Good overview of events leading the war.

Battle of Lexington
http://odur.let.rug.nl/~usa/E/lexington/lexingxx.htm
Good overview with links to biographies.

Battle of Concord
http://odur.let.rug.nl/~usa/E/concord/concorxx.htm
Good overview with links to biographies.

Index